AN INSTANT GUIDE TO

DINOSAURS & PREHISTORIC LIFE

Fascinating plants and animals
that lived on earth before mankind
described and illustrated in full color

Pamela Forey

CRESCENT BOOKS
NEW YORK • AVENEL, NEW JERSEY

This 1988 edition published by Crescent Books, distributed
by Outlet Book Company, Inc., a Random House Company,
40 Engelhard Avenue, Avenel, New Jersey 07001.

Random House
New York • Toronto • London • Sydney • Auckland

Manufactured in Malaysia

ISBN: 0-517-66218-3

10 9 8 7 6 5

Contents

Introduction

The animals and plants that have lived on this Earth during the millions of years of its history are strange and unfamiliar in many respects. This book provides a fascinating glimpse of life in bygone ages, from the early animals that lived in the seas of the Cambrian period, 550 million years ago to the great woolly mammoths and other mammals that lived in the last Ice Age, only a few thousand years ago. It describes the fishes that lived in the seas before there was any life on land, the strange plants of the Coal Age swamps, the great dinosaurs that roamed the Earth 100 million years ago, and the often grotesque mammals that followed them, after the dinosaurs had died out.

How to use this book

We have divided the book into eight sections, all but the first of these based on the biology of the organisms. The sections are: **The History of the Earth**; **Ancient Plants**; **Invertebrate Animals**; **Fishes**; **Amphibians**; **Reptiles**; **Mammals**; and **Birds**. Each section is indicated by a different color band at the top of each page (see *Contents Page*.)

The History of the Earth. This section consists of one large illustration which summarizes the history of the Earth, from its formation 4500 million years ago to the present day. Included here are the names of the eras and periods into which the history of our planet is divided and which are referred to extensively in the rest of the text, together with their ages and time spans.   **14–15**

Ancient Plants. This section begins with the most ancient life forms known, the stromatolites formed by algae in the Precambrian era. It continues with descriptions of the earliest land plants, the plants of the great coal forests and the earliest seed-forming plants.   **16–23**

Invertebrate Animals are those which lack backbones. They were the earliest animals to appear (the earliest forms appeared in the Precambrian) and still in terms of numbers, they far outnumber the larger, and perhaps more familiar, vertebrate animals. They include animals with widely diverse features which are described on the relevant pages in the text.

Some are illustrated in the Glossary pages 12–13 to show characteristic features mentioned in the text. Included here are the Foraminifera; Sponges; Corals; Bryozoa; Mollusks (including ammonoids, nautiloids, belemnoids, gastropods and pelycepods); Brachiopods; Arthropods (including trilobites, eurypterids and insects); Echinoderms (including sea lilies, sea urchins, cystoids, blastoids, sea stars and brittlestars); and Graptolites. **24–45**

Early Fishes. Fishes first appeared in Silurian times but became common for the first time in the Devonian. They live in water and have streamlined bodies, tails used for swimming, and fins. Early ones had a variable number of fins, but later fishes had a fixed pattern of dorsal, anal and paired fins, illustrated in the Glossary. Their bodies were covered in scales or bony armor. **46–55**

Early Amphibians. Amphibians first appeared in Devonian times, evolving from fishes, probably from rhipidistians. They lived on land and breathed air, had four limbs with four or more digits on each foot. But their stance was ungainly and sprawling, they had moist skin and we assume that they laid their eggs in water. Many were quite large. **56–59**

Reptiles evolved from amphibians in the Carboniferous. They became a highly successful and diverse group, which included primitive reptiles, turtles, plesiosaurs and other marine reptiles, dinosaurs, pterosaurs and mammal-like reptiles. Typically, they had scale-covered skins, were well adapted to life on land and presumably laid large leathery eggs, like those of modern reptiles. Probably many of the marine and mammal-like reptiles bore live young. It is thought that some of them, the dinosaurs for instance, may have been warm-blooded. **60–88**

Mammals evolved from mammal-like reptiles in the Triassic. They differed from the closest of their reptilian ancestors in the possession of a single bone in the jaw. They had fur, we assume they were warm-blooded and bore their young alive. Mesozoic mammals were small and insignificant and the mammals did not become dominant land animals until the Tertiary, after the dinosaurs had died out. **89–118**

Birds evolved from dinosaur-like ancestors in the Jurassic. They have light skeletons, feathers, wings and a distinctive opposable digit on each hind foot. **119–121**

What's on a page

On most pages only one species is described and there are four boxes of information about the animal or plant illustrated. The characteristic features of the organism are described in the first box, speculation about its biology in the second, the time it lived and where it is found today in the third, and similar and related species in the fourth.

On some pages, particularly in the Invertebrate Animals and Fishes sections, a group of plants or animals is described, e.g. rugose corals or pteraspid fishes. In some cases the group is described on a double page spread, with a general description on the left page and examples on the right.

Specimen Page

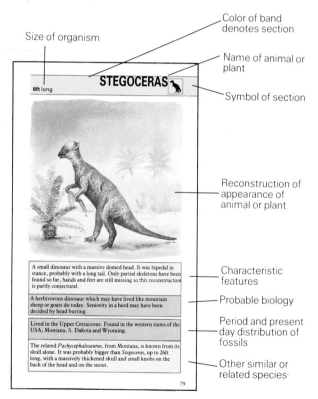

Color of band denotes section

Size of organism

Name of animal or plant

Symbol of section

Reconstruction of appearance of animal or plant

Characteristic features

Probable biology

Period and present day distribution of fossils

Other similar or related species·

6ft long

STEGOCERAS

A small dinosaur with a massive domed head. It was bipedal in stance, probably with a long tail. Only partial skeletons have been found so far, hands and feet are still missing so this reconstruction is partly conjectural.

A herbivorous dinosaur which may have lived like mountain sheep or goats do today. Seniority in a herd may have been decided by head butting.

Lived in the Upper Cretaceous. Found in the western states of the USA; Montana, S. Dakota and Wyoming.

The related *Pachycephalosaurus*, from Montana, is known from its skull alone. It was probably bigger than *Stegoceras*, up to 26ft long, with a massively thickened skull and small knobs on the back of the head and on the snout.

79

The illustration on most pages is a reconstruction of the animal or plant. The colors in the reconstructions are speculative. In some cases, especially in the Invertebrate Animals section, the fossils themselves are illustrated.

You may be frustrated by the lack of consistency in the information about these organisms. It may seem to you that facts are omitted which should be included. This is usually because the information is simply not available. Animals and plants are rarely fossilized intact; their remains consist only of the hard parts like bones and shells, or of impressions in the rocks. The skeletons of vertebrates are often broken up before fossilization, and often we do not know what, for example, their feet, or hands, or tails looked like, for they have never been found.

What fossils reveal

The section on the biology of the animal or plant is necessarily speculative, based on the kinds of rocks they are preserved in, the associations of the organisms and comparisons with living relatives. For instance, rocks which contain fishes are formed in water, therefore other organisms present either lived in the water or fell in at death. It is usually possible to tell whether water-formed rocks were laid down in the sea, in lakes or in rivers. Organisms in marine rocks are unlikely to have fallen in, whereas riverine rocks contain both aquatic and terrestrial organisms. Comparison with living organisms can be helpful in determining feeding habits, e.g. vertebrates can be classed as carnivores or herbivores, depending on the kind of teeth they have.

In the third box the period in which the animal or plant lived and the present day distribution of its fossils are described. The configuration of land and sea have not always been the same as they are today. Three giant continents, called Gondwanaland, Laurasia and Angaraland existed in the Paleozoic and they moved relative to each other, finally drifting together to form one supercontinent, called Pangaea, during the Permian. This existed throughout the Triassic, after which time the continents separated and drifted until they reached their present configuration. The movement of the continents affected the climates and the distribution of the plants and animals that lived on and around them. Present day distributions of fossils reflect the positions of the continents in the periods when the animals or plants lived.

Illustrated Glossary

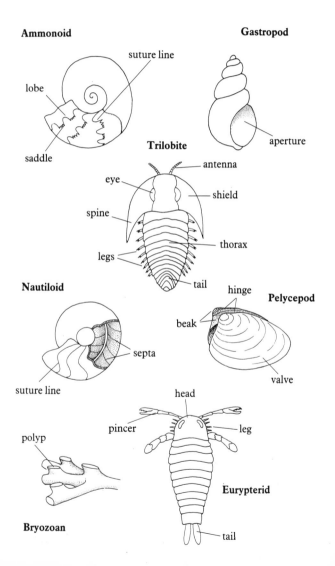

Ammonoid
- suture line
- lobe
- saddle

Gastropod
- aperture

Trilobite
- antenna
- eye
- shield
- spine
- thorax
- legs
- tail

Nautiloid
- septa
- suture line

Pelycepod
- hinge
- beak
- valve

Eurypterid
- head
- pincer
- leg
- tail

Bryozoan
- polyp

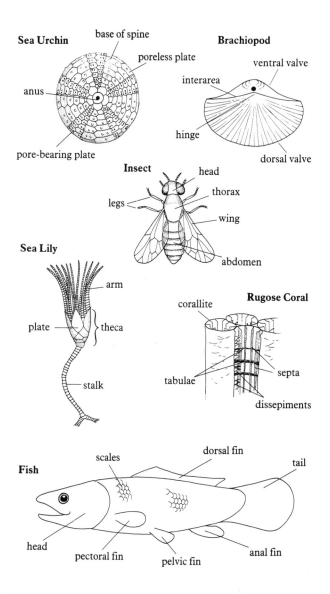

SYSTEM	PERIOD	LIFE FORMS
Cenozoic	Quaternary	
	Tertiary	
Mesozoic (Age of Dinosaurs)	Cretaceous	
	Jurassic	
	Triassic	
Paleozoic	Permian	
	Carboniferous	
	Devonian (Age of fishes)	
	Silurian	
	Ordovician	
	Cambrian (Trilobites)	
Precambrian		

HISTORY OF THE EARTH

EPOCH	SIGNIFICANT EVENTS	AGE
Recent	Ice retreats to present position	
Pleistocene (Ice Age)	Ice covers much of Europe & N. America	2
Pliocene	Climate becomes colder. Many mammals become extinct. Appearance of man	6
Miocene	Rise & spread of grasslands, associated with spread of grazing mammals	22
Oligocene	Many early mammals become extinct	36
Eocene **Paleocene**	Early mammals diversify. Appearance of many modern mammal groups	65
	Many animals become extinct, incl. dinosaurs & ammonites. Rise of flowering plants	145
	Peak of dinosaur diversity. Rise of birds	210
	Reptiles diversify rapidly. First mammals appear	250
	Widespread extinction of marine animals. Mammal-like reptiles diversify	290
Pennsylvanian (Coal Age)	Coal swamps with lush vegetation. Rise of winged insects & primitive reptiles	340
Mississippian	Widespread shallow seas with reefs. Amphibians diversify	365
	Widespread invasion of fresh water by animals & plants. Rise of ammonoids in sea. Fishes diversify	415
	Rise of land plants. Prolific life in shallow seas	465
	Spread of shallow seas over land. Marine invertebrates diversify rapidly	510
	Many animals developed hard skeletons	575
	Soft bodied animals & algae present, incl. stromatolites	
	Development of free oxygen	3000
	Birth of planet Earth	4600

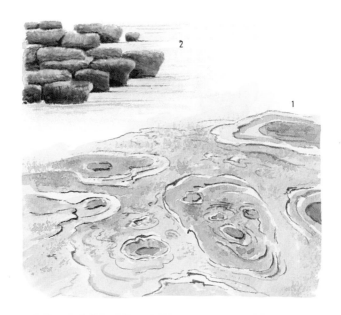

One of the earliest kinds of fossils in the Earth's history, and often massive. They consist of domes or columns, flat "biscuits" or mats in the rocks. They were probably produced by blue-green algae and bacteria, since fossilized cells resembling these organisms can be seen in the stromatolites.

The algae which formed the stromatolites probably grew in shallow seas, on mud flats or in lakes. Modern stromatolites are rare because the algae are grazed by invertebrates.

First appeared in the fossil record in the Precambrian, 3000 million years ago and still occur. The fossils are found worldwide.

No similar fossils. One of the oldest and largest occurs in Wyoming, others are found in Ontario and Montana. The illustration shows a mat-like fossilized stromatolite (**1**) and a reconstruction of what it might have looked like in life, (**2**) based on a modern stromatolite from Australia.

A small plant with prostrate stems from which grew "roots" and erect green leafless stems, smooth and cylindrical in shape. These branched dichotomously and bore terminal egg-shaped sporangia.

One of the earliest land plants. The plants grew in tidal mud flats and swampy areas.

Lived in Lower Devonian times. Found in the Rhynie Chert Bed in Scotland. Probably preserved *in situ*, since they are fossilized upright.

Cooksonia, the earliest land plant known to date, was similar and also grew on tidal mud flats; it was only 3in tall. It is found throughout the world in Silurian rocks. *Zosterophyllum* was also similar but had many radially arranged sporangia terminating side branches on the stems.

LEPIDODENDRON

Up to **100ft** tall

1

A large tree-like plant, with a single, trunk-sized stem covered with overlapping leaf bases; these form the most frequent fossils (**1**.) The stem terminated in many dichotomous branches, clothed with spirally arranged leaves and ending in cones. The base of the stem had many dichotomously branched roots.

These trees grew in swampy areas in dense forests. The land was gradually sinking and the forests were periodically covered by the sea.

Lived in the Mississippian. The plant remains did not rot when the forests were inundated and they formed peat; this gradually became coal. Found in Europe and N. America.

Sigillaria was similar but the leaf bases on its stem were arranged in vertical rows. It had only one or two branches at the top of its stem and long grass-like leaves. It is found in the same areas as *Lepidodendron*.

1

Jointed underground stems grew horizontally, rooting from the joints. From these grew tall tree-like stems, also jointed and with many branches growing from their joints. The branches bore whorls of linear leaves so that they resembled giant bottle brushes (**1**.) Whorls of cones grew in the leaf axils.

These trees grew in swampy areas in dense forests. The land was gradually sinking and the forests were periodically covered by the sea.

Lived in the Mississippian. The plant remains did not rot when the forests were inundated and they formed peat; this gradually became coal. Found in Europe and N. America.

There were other similar plants living at the same time, which had fewer, irregular branches or only two branches at each joint. Related plants are the smaller horsetails, species of which are still living.

Plants with woody, tree-like trunks covered with old leaf bases. The trunk was topped with fern-like fronds and had roots at its base. Large seeds were borne on the fronds.

These tree-like plants grew in swampy areas in dense forests. The land was gradually sinking and the forests were periodically covered by the sea.

Lived from Pennsylvanian to Permian times, but most numerous in coal of the Mississippian. Found in Coal Measures of N. America and Europe. The leaves are the most common remains.

Medullosa (illustrated) was the most common of the seed ferns. *Caytonia* was probably related to these plants; it is known from seeds and palmate leaves in Mesozoic rocks of N. America and Europe. Its stems have not been identified.

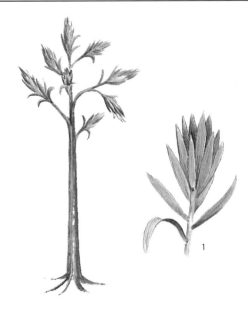

1

A tall tree with many branches. The strap-shaped leaves had parallel veins; they grew in a spiral arrangement on the branches, as shown in (**1**.) Cones grew in the leaf axils. The roots were probably stilt-like in appearance.

These trees probably grew in swamps, along estuaries and coastlines, rather like mangroves do today. The swamps later formed coal.

Lived from early Carboniferous to Permian times. Found in Asia, India, Australia, S. Africa, N. and S. America. Some coal balls contain nothing but these plants.

Glossopteris leaves have a central midrib and a network of veins. Conifers have needle-like or scale-like leaves.

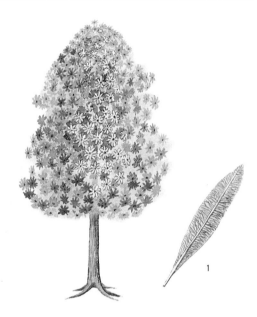

1

A tree-like plant. Its tongue-shaped leaves (**1**) had a central midrib and a network of veins; they grew in whorls or spirals on short shoots. Seeds and pollen organs have been found with the leaves. The roots of the tree had characteristic wedge-shaped veins in the center.

Dominant plants of Gondwanaland, which formed a huge continent in the southern hemisphere at the time. They grew in large swamps, which later formed coal.

Lived in Permian times and found in rocks of this period throughout the southern hemisphere. Less common in Triassic rocks. The leaves are the most common fossils.

Other similar plants, like *Gangamopteris* which had larger leaves, also grew in Gondwanaland at the time. The leaves of the unrelated, but also common, **Cordaites** have parallel veins.

22

This plant had a globular trunk, covered with old, spirally arranged leaf bases embedded in flat, tongue-shaped scales. The trunk was topped by a crown of compound leaves. The large cones, which grew on the trunk, resembled flowers and may have had nectaries to attract insects.

These plants were widely distributed and abundant in the Mesozoic.

Lived in Jurassic and Cretaceous times, most common in the Jurassic. Found in Europe, N. America and India. Many fossils have been found in the Black Hills of S. Dakota.

Cycads (a few species of which still survive) have similar leaves. They can be distinguished from *Cycadeoidea* by anatomical details in the leaves, especially in the stomata (air holes.)

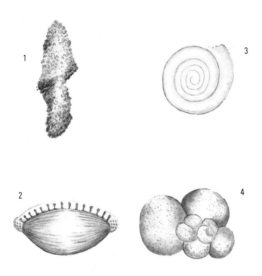

One-celled animals, most with multilocular tests (shells) although early forms had unilocular tests. They vary in shape from tubes and flasks to disks, coils, stars, roses, valves and plaits. The tests may be made of particles stuck together but are more often calcareous or siliceous.

Most forams have lived at the bottom of the sea, and are common in rocks formed in deep sea sediments. Others have been planktonic. A few live in fresh water.

Lived from Cambrian to Recent times and still common in all the oceans. They are important as stratigraphic indexers and in the detection of oil-bearing rocks.

Most forams have been microscopic although a few species have been larger, their tests measuring nearly an inch across.
Illustrated are (**1**) *Rabosommina*, Ordovician; (**2**) *Fusulinella*, Pennsylvanian; (**3**) *Cormispira*, Carboniferous-Recent.; (**4**) *Globigerina*, Cretaceous-Recent.

24

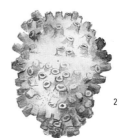

Colonial attached animals with calcareous or siliceous skeletons, the skeleton formed of spicules or a rigid framework. Their fossils may be of many forms, cup-like, flask-like, tubular or encrusting. They are covered with many tiny pores and also have one or more larger openings.

Almost all sponges lived in the sea, on rocks or on shells of other animals. Water, bringing oxygen and food, enters through the tiny pores and leaves by the larger openings.

All three groups of sponges originated in Cambrian times and are still living today. Their fossils are found in marine rocks all over the world.

Siliceous sponges, like *Ventriculites* (**1**) are common in Paleozoic and Mesozoic rocks, and their skeletons provided silica for the formation of flints and chert. Calcareous sponges, like *Peridonella* (**2**) were important reef builders in Permian and Triassic times. Desmosponges are rare in the fossil record.

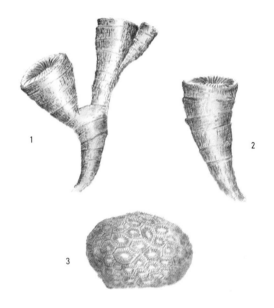

1

2

3

Simple or colonial corals with a wrinkled surface. Solitary ones were horn-shaped, others were branching, massive or encrusting. Inside each corallite there were many radial vertical divisions (septa) and horizontal divisions (tabulae) as well as slanting divisions near the walls (dissepiments.)

Many of these were important reef builders in Silurian and Devonian seas. Their colonies grew by branching or becoming massive; individual colonies grew up to 12in across.

Lived in Paleozoic times, becoming extinct at the end of the Permian. Found in marine rocks all over the world.

Heliophyllum (**1,**) from the Devonian was a branched form. *Caninia* (**2,**) from Pennsylvanian-Permian, was solitary. *Lonsdaleia* (**3,**) from the Carboniferous and *Hexagonaria* (Devonian) were massive colonial forms in which the coral buds remained in close contact with each other.

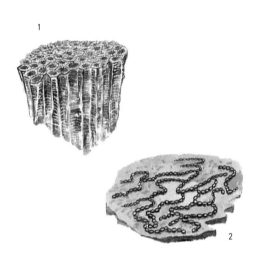

Colonial corals with no septa (or septa reduced to ridges) and no dissepiments. They have tubular corallites often crowded together like a honeycomb or forming a mat. In many species, individual corallites are divided internally from wall to wall by horizontal tabulae, but in some tabulae are missing.

These were important reef-building corals in the Silurian and Devonian periods.

Lived from the Ordovician to the end of the Permian. Found in marine rocks worldwide.

Favosites (**1**) was a massive coral from the Silurian and Devonian; its corallites were prismatic in shape with many tabulae. Its many species are found in N. America and Europe. *Halysites* (**2**) formed chains of elongated corallites; it is found worldwide in Ordovician and Silurian rocks.

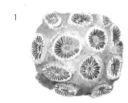

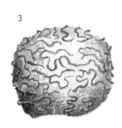

Solitary or colonial corals. There are many radial divisions (septa) and a central rod-like or spongy rod inside each individual corallite. Many also have dissepiments but they do not have horizontal divisions (tabulae.)

The reef-building corals of modern oceans are all members of this group. A large coral may be over a hundred years old, but the living part represents only a thin film on the surface.

Lived from the beginning of the Mesozoic and still common today. Their fossils are found in marine rocks worldwide.

Favia (**1**) has been an important reef builder since the Cretaceous; it forms massive, encrusting or tubular colonies. *Acropora* (**2**) has formed branching colonies since the Eocene. *Meandrina* (**3**) is the Brain Coral, with many elongated corallites. It first appeared in the Eocene.

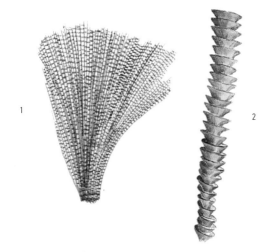

Colonial animals forming moss-like encrustations, funnels, lumps or branched tree-like forms. They consist of tiny "polyps" contained in walls, many joined together to form one colony. The walls are made of protein, impregnated with calcite and it is these which form the fossils.

Marine animals; the colonies are attached to other animals or to rocks. They are and were most common on the continental shelf in shallow sunlit seas.

Lived from Ordovician times to the present day. Found in marine rocks worldwide. Often occur in limestones where they may be so abundant that they form the bulk of the rock.

Fenestella (**1**) resembles modern day species which encrust seaweeds; it is found in Ordovician to Permian rocks in Europe. Bryozoans of the genus *Archimedes* (**2**) are known as Archimedes' screws; they are found in Carboniferous and Permian rocks throughout the northern hemisphere.

Mollusks with shells spirally coiled in one plane. Shells are divided internally into many chambers, the dividing walls (septa) either smoothly lobed or resembling elaborate tracings. These septa show up as suture lines where they meet the outside walls of the shell.

Marine oceanic organisms. The animal lived in the chamber nearest the aperture; its head and tentacles projected outside the shell; the rest of the shell formed a buoyancy device.

Lived from Devonian to Cretaceous times. Fossils are internal molds of the shell. One of the commonest fossils worldwide, they are widely used for correlation of rocks in stratigraphy.

Goniatites (**1**,) which lived from mid Devonian to Triassic, had saddles and lobes on the suture lines, but these were smooth and undivided. In *Ceratites* (**2**,) which lived in the Triassic, the saddles were entire but the lobes were divided or serrated.

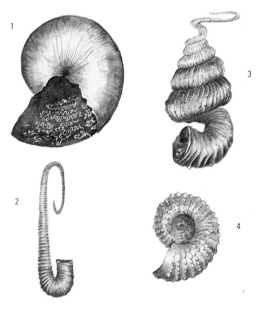

The ammonites were the most successful of the ammonoids. In these mollusks, both the saddles & the lobes of the suture lines were greatly subdivided to form ornate, feathery patterns. Some of these mollusks were tiny, others grew up to 3ft across. They lived in the sea, mostly in water over 100ft deep with a sandy or muddy bottom. They lived from the Triassic to the end of the Cretaceous when they became extinct like so many other animals. *Phylloceras* (1) was a typical ammonite. It is found in Jurassic and Cretaceous rocks throughout the world.

During the course of their history, ammonites assumed some strange forms. *Hamites* (2,) which lived in the Cretaceous, was a form in which the shell was uncoiled. Its fossils are found in Europe, N. America, Africa & Asia. The shell of *Helicoceras* (3) was only partly coiled. It is found in the Cretaceous of the USA. Others retained the coiled shells but their shells became ornamented with ribs & tubercles; such is *Douvilleiceras* (4,) found in Cretaceous rocks in much of the world.

Mollusks with chambered shells. In early forms the shells were almost straight but some later forms evolved shells coiled in one plane. Shells were mostly smooth and the septa and suture lines formed broad unlobed curves. Some Ordovician forms grew up to 9ft long.

Marine animals which crawled on sandy bottoms in offshore waters or floated in the ocean. Head and tentacles projected from the body chamber. The shell acted as a buoyancy device.

Lived from Upper Cambrian to the present day. Fossils are world wide in marine rocks but most common in the Ordovician. Fossilized as internal molds that show the suture line.

The illustration shows a reconstruction of the straight-shelled *Orthoceros* (**1**) and *Gigantoceras* (**2**,) which had a coiled shell: both these nautiloids lived in the Paleozoic. Other nautiloids, *Cyrtoceras* for example, had curved shells.

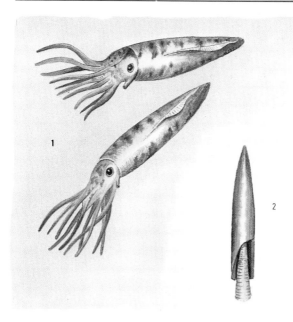

1

2

Squid-like, torpedo-shaped mollusks. The only part which is fossilized is the internal skeleton. This consisted of a bullet-shaped object (the guard) the blunt, front end of which surrounded the reduced chambered shell. The shell extended forwards to protect the body.

Marine animals with two lateral fins, a large head with well-developed eyes and ten tentacles with many hooks. The guard served as a ballast device. They swam by jet propulsion.

Lived from Carboniferous to the Oligocene, but best known in Jurassic and Cretaceous, where they are used as indicators. Worldwide. Some fossils have retained impressions of flesh.

The illustration shows a reconstruction of *Cylindroteuthis* (**1**,) a belemnoid that lived in Jurassic and Cretaceous times and is found in N. America and Europe. The fossilized guard and shell (**2**) are oval in cross section and about 6in long. Other belemnoid guards vary in size and in shape.

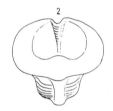

Many early snails had uncoiled shells but some were coiled in one plane. Most later forms had spirally coiled shells, often with an operculum over the aperture. Many are decorated by spiral lines or axial ribs and others have spines. They vary in shape from rounded shells to turrets and cones.

Marine, freshwater and terrestrial mollusks; carnivores and herbivores. Land snails first appeared in the Carboniferous. The body fills the shell and projects through the aperture.

Lived from the early Cambrian to the present day. Common fossils in many rocks throughout the world, but not much used in stratigraphy.

Bellerophon (**1**,) which is found worldwide, lived from Silurian to Triassic times; it had a smooth globular shell with a deep slit in the front margin of the aperture (**2**.) *Turritella* (**3**) appeared in the Cretaceous and still lives today. **Ammonoids** have shells coiled in one plane and sutures on the shells.

PELYCEPODS

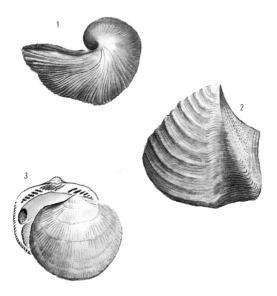

Mollusks with shells formed of two equal, hinged valves which are mostly mirror images of each other. Each valve has a beak over the hinge; in many the beak is nearer the front end of the shell than the hind end. Hinge formation is variable. The shells are smooth or ornamented by spines or ribs.

Marine and freshwater animals which live attached to rocks, or burrow into sand or mud. They feed by drawing water into the shell and filtering out organisms in the water.

Lived from mid Cambrian to the present day. Worldwide. Important stratigraphic indicators, especially in Coal Measures, Cretaceous and Tertiary.

Gryphaea (**1**) was an oyster that lived in Triassic and Jurassic seas; similar forms were found in the Cretaceous. *Trigonia* (**2**) was a distinctive pelycepod that lived from the Triassic to the Cretaceous. Fossilized *Glycimeris* (**3**) shells form extensive shell beds. All occur in rocks throughout the world.

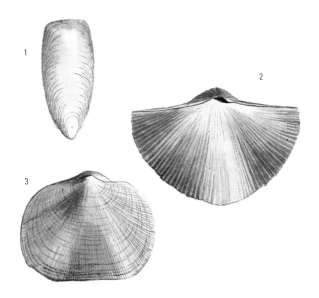

Animals with a shell formed of two valves. The valves are often domed and asymmetrical, the ventral valve being larger than the dorsal valve. The valves of most species are joined by a central hinge consisting of two teeth on the ventral valve which fit into sockets on the dorsal valve.

Marine animals which live in shallow sunlit seas. Many are attached to rocks by their stalks, others live on sandy bottoms and lose their stalks, becoming partly buried.

Lived from Cambrian times to the present day. Most common from the Ordovician to Carboniferous, and during the Jurassic. Only about 220 species live today. Found in rocks worldwide.

Lingula (**1**) and related brachiopods have no hinge, the valves are held together by muscles. *Lingula* appeared in the Cambrian and is still alive today. All other brachiopods have hinges. Most **Bivalve** mollusk shells have two identical valves and the hinge is often displaced toward the front of the shell.

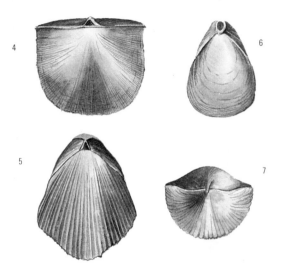

Spiriferid Brachiopods

eg. *Spirifer* (**2** on opposite page) often had winged shells. Mid Ordovician-Jurassic.

Orthid Brachiopods

eg. *Schizophoria* (**3** on opposite page) had broad biconvex shells. The hinge line was long. Interareas visible on both valves. Cambrian-Permian.

Strophomenid Brachiopods

eg. *Strophomena* (**4**) had one convex & one concave valve. Hinge line was wide. Interareas visible on both valves. Ordovician-Recent, only common in Devonian.

Pentamerid Brachiopods

eg. *Conchidium* (**5**) were biconvex with a short hinge line. Interareas visible on both valves. Silurian-Devonian.

Terebratulid Brachiopods

eg. *Dielasma* (**6**) have smooth shells with interarea visible only on ventral valve, if at all. Silurian-Recent.

Rhynchonellid Brachiopods

eg. *Hypothyridina* (**7**) are wedge-shaped with a U-shaped curve in the line between the valves. Shells are ridged & interareas very small. Ordovician-Recent.

Arthropods, divided longitudinally into three sections. They had a head-like shield region, often with bizarre spines, antennae and eyes which varied from simple dots to crescent-shaped, compound structures. The body consisted of segmented thorax and tail, each segment bearing a pair of legs.

Marine animals, most common in sandy shallow seas. They molted as they grew and some fossils represent molts rather than whole animals. They could roll into a ball for defence.

Lived from early Cambrian to Permian times, reaching a peak in the Ordovician. Only a few survived into the Carboniferous and Permian. Found in marine rocks worldwide.

The illustration shows the trilobite, **Phacops**, as it might have appeared in life (**1**.) It lived in the Silurian and Devonian periods and is found throughout the world. *Phacops* could roll into a ball to defend itself against predators (**2**) and is often found fossilized in this position.

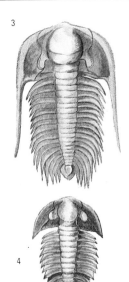

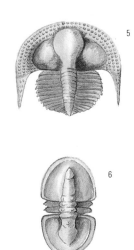

Paradoxides (3)

Head much larger than tail. There are large eyes & long spines on sides of head. Central part of head has three cross furrows. Thorax about 18 segments, with spines on edges of segments. Cambrian of N. America, Europe, Africa & Australia.

Olenoides (4)

Head & tail about the same size. Eyes medium-sized. Short spines on edges of head. Thorax about 7 segments with spines on the edges of the segments. Cambrian of N. & S. America, Asia.

Cryptolithus (5)

Head very much larger than tail, about half the length of the organism. Wide front border of head has rows of radiating pits & there are long spines on sides of head. Eyes absent. Thorax about 6 segments. Ordovician. N. America & Europe.

Triplognathus (6)

Less than half an inch long. Head & tail similar, eyes absent. Thorax only 2 segments. One of many similar very small trilobites. Cambrian. N. America, Europe, Asia & Australia.

Elongated arthropods with segmented bodies, a shield-like head and a spine-like or paddle-like tail. They had five pairs of legs, and many also had a pair of pincers.

Early forms were marine, later forms invaded brackish lagoons and fresh water. They crawled over the bottom or swam with a paddle-like tail. They were probably ferocious predators.

Lived from Ordovician to Permian times. Found in N. America, Europe and Asia.

Eurypterus (illustrated) lived in the Silurian. It had tiny pincers; four of its pairs of legs were spiny and used for walking while the last pair were used as paddles. *Pterygotus* grew up to 6ft long; it was a dangerous animal with long, toothed pincers. It lived in late Silurian and early Devonian.

Insects have three sections to the body — head, thorax and abdomen and three pairs of legs. Primitive wingless insects appeared in mid Devonian, winged insects resembling giant dragonflies and beetles in the Pennsylvanian. Insects like flies, moths and butterflies appeared in the Permian.

Early winged insects lived in the lush vegetation of the coal swamps. Flowering plants appeared in the Cretaceous, and their long association with insects began.

Lived from Devonian to the present day. Insects do not fossilize well except in fine-grained rocks like coal or lithographic limestone. The best fossils are found in amber.

Insects like *Meganeura* (**1,**) which resembled a giant dragonfly, flew over the coal swamps. It had a wingspan of up to 30in and its body was 15in long. This fly is embedded in amber (**2,**) which is fossilized tree resin.

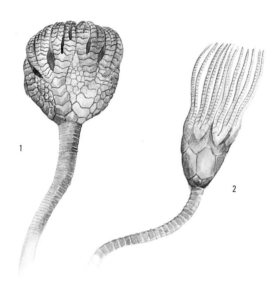

Pentamerous plant-like echinoderms with a cup-shaped body (theca) and five simple or usually branched arms. Most have a segmented stalk with a root-like or disk-like attachment organ at the base. The theca is formed of plates which are connected to the arm plates and the mouth of the animal is at the top.

Sea lilies lived attached by their stalks in shallow seas. Recent stalked crinoids live in deeper waters while feather stars (stalkless forms) live in shallow offshore waters.

Lived from Lower Ordovician to the present day. Their fossils, often the stalk segments only, are found worldwide and may form the bulk of some limestones (crinoidal limestone.)

Crinoids lived in huge numbers in Devonian to Carboniferous times and crinoidal limestones may form beds 200ft thick. *Taxocrinus* (**1**) has a theca made of many loose plates. *Platycrinites* (**2**) has a theca formed of a few tightly joined plates. Both come from rocks of N. America and Europe.

SEA URCHINS

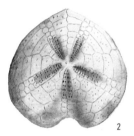

Spherical, flattened or heart-shaped echinoderms, covered with plates arranged in a regular pentamerous pattern. The symmetry comes from five radiating double rows of pore-bearing plates, separated by double rows of poreless plates. The plates bear spines in life, of which only the bases may be preserved.

Marine benthic animals living in shallow offshore waters, in deep water and on reefs. They may cling to rocks with their spines, live in holes or in quiet sandy waters.

Lived from Ordovician times to the present day. Found in rocks worldwide, they are important indicators in Jurassic, Cretaceous and Tertiary rocks.

In circular echinoids, like *Hemicidaris* (**1**) the anus is at the apex of the animal with the mouth beneath. *Hemicidaris* had large spines, and the bases remain on the fossil. Irregular echinoids, like *Micraster* (**2**) have heart-shaped, pentagonal or irregular bodies, in which the anus is not at the apex.

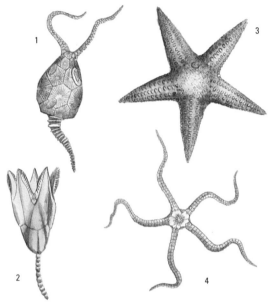

Cystoids (1)
Vase-like or spherical echinoderms covered by many calcareous plates; many had short stalks, some had arms. Two to five fine radiating grooves led to the mouth. Ordovician-Carboniferous; less common after the Silurian.

Blastoids (2)
Rigid bud-like animals on short stalks. Bud had five deep, cross-ribbed grooves separated by five V-shaped plates. Many arms lined the grooves, but these are usually missing in fossils. Devonian-Permian; most common in Carboniferous.

Sea Stars (3)
Flattened star-shaped animals covered with calcareous plates & with five or more broad-based arms. Five grooves run along undersides of arms. Mouth on undersurface of body. Lower Ordovician-Recent, but fossils most common in Devonian shales.

Brittlestars (4)
Similar animals to sea stars but with a central disk & long narrow arms, attached to disk by a narrow base. Lower Ordovician-Recent, but fossils most common in Devonian shales.

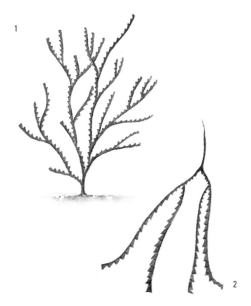

Colonial animals composed of threads on which were many minute cups, giving the threads a serrated appearance. Early forms were net-like but later forms were simpler with only a few dichotomously branched threads. In some the cups were on one side of the thread only, in others they were on both sides.

Marine animals, many of which were planktonic, floating in the surface waters. The early net-like forms were usually attached to other objects.

Lived in Cambrian to Carboniferous times. Fossilized as fine silvery carbon or pyrite lines on black shales. Useful stratigraphic markers, since they changed rapidly through time.

Dendrograptus (**1**) is a net-like form found in Cambrian to Carboniferous rocks worldwide. *Tetragraptus* (**2**) is found in Ordovician rocks throughout much of the world. It consisted of four short branches with cups on one side of the threads only. Other graptolites had from one to many branches.

PTERASPID FISHES

6–16in long

Small torpedo-shaped fishes with pointed snouts. The rear of the body was covered with lozenge-shaped scales and there was a shield over the front of the body and the head. They had no fins, a tiny jawless mouth beneath the head, and two tiny eyes on the sides of the head with a third eye on top of the head.

Most lived in rivers, probably at the bottom. They fed on small organisms which they caught with a series of small plates around the mouth. These plates functioned as a scoop.

Lived in Lower Devonian times. They are found in both marine and freshwater Devonian rocks of North America and Europe.

Pteraspis (illustrated) comes from Europe. It was about 10in long with an oval shield. Some pteraspids, like *Drepanaspis* (from Europe) had disk-shaped shields; others, like *Doryaspis* (also from Europe) had long spines on their sides.

About **12in** long

Small fishes, with heads encased in broad, semi-circular shields and spines covering backs and sides. They had patches of sensory scales on the shields. Their eyes were close together on the top of the head, with a third eye between. They had a dorsal fin, pectoral fins and an upturned tail.

Most lived on the bottom in lakes and rivers, where they probably fed on small organisms in the mud. They sucked in the mud through their small jawless mouths.

Lived from late Silurian to late Devonian times. Found in both marine and freshwater rocks, in North America and Europe.

Cephalaspis (illustrated) comes from the Devonian of Europe. Other species differ mostly in the shape of the head shield and in the length of the spines. *Boreaspis* (from Europe) had an elongated snout. *Tremataspis* (from Europe) had no spines or pectoral fins.

47

Elongated fishes with upturned tails and small heads. The head and front part of the body was enclosed in box-like armor, made of interlocking plates. The head shield articulated with the body through a ball-and-socket joint. The pectoral fins were replaced by bony "arms." The mouth possessed weak jaws.

Antiarchs lived in fresh water and, less commonly, in marine environments. They probably fed on small animals like prawns and shrimps.

Lived from mid Silurian to late Devonian times and found throughout the world in rocks of this age.

Bothriolepis (illustrated) lived in rivers, lakes and coastal waters. Its fossils occur in mid and Upper Devonian rocks throughout the world. Its bony arms may have been used to prop the body up or anchor it against currents. *Pterichthyodes* had a scaly body and stronger arms. It comes from Europe.

48

Elongated, scaleless fishes with head and trunk encased in heavy bony shields. A complicated neck joint allowed the skull to be rotated upwards while the lower jaw was dropped, giving the fishes a wide gape. The head was large with large eyes and the jaws contained blade-like shearing teeth.

Arthrodires were numerous both in fresh water and in the sea. Most were probably sluggish predatory fishes which lived near the bottom of the water.

Lived in the Devonian. Found in marine and freshwater rocks of this age throughout the world.

Dinichthys (illustrated) was a large marine arthrodire, about 25ft long; it preyed on other fishes. It comes from Upper Devonian rocks of Ohio, N. America. *Coccosteus* was similar but much smaller (only about 18in long;) it lived in fresh water and is found in Devonian rocks in Europe.

Streamlined fishes with slightly pointed snouts and a deep powerful tail. The mouth is positioned beneath the head; it is long with a wide gape and equipped with many hundreds of teeth. The body is covered with a barely visible shagreen of tiny scales. Males have claspers on pelvic fins.

Marine predatory fishes, feeding mostly on other fishes. These are fast swimmers; modern sharks have no positive buoyancy and have to swim constantly, presumably ancient ones did too.

Lived from late Devonian until the present day, and still common. Sharks' teeth are common fossils in marine rocks throughout the world.

Sharks vary in the shapes of their teeth, in the lengths of the snouts and in tail shape. *Stethacanthus* (illustrated,) comes from Mississippian rocks of N. America and Europe. It grew to 20in long, had a front dorsal fin modified into a brush-like organ and long trailing edges on the pectoral fins.

ACANTHODIAN FISHES

Streamlined fishes, covered with tiny, closely fitting scales. They had blunt snouts, large eyes and long jaws. All the fins except the tail, had a prominent spine at the front from which the fin extended backward like a sail.

Freshwater fishes which lived in lakes and swamps. Most had teeth and were predators but others (like *Acanthodes*) fed by straining small organisms from the water with the gill rakers.

Lived from Silurian to Lower Permian times. Found in rocks of this age throughout the world. Some, like *Acanthodes* are abundant in the Pennsylvanian Coal Measures.

Acanthodes (illustrated) is found in N. America and Europe. It had no teeth but its gills were equipped with a comb of rakers. *Climatius* (Lower Devonian of Europe) had thick ornamented spines on its fins; it was a predator with many teeth in its jaws.

51

These fishes had short snouts, long jaws and large eyes. The streamlined body was covered with shiny, ornamented, rhomboid scales, interlocking to form a tough coat of armor. The head was covered with ornamented bones. The fins had bony fin rays and a leading edge made of tiny knife-like scales.

Marine and freshwater fishes. These were active predators, with large eyes for detecting prey and many needle-like teeth in the jaws.

Lived in Silurian to Cretaceous times. Found in rocks throughout the world.

A large group of fishes which varied from the Scottish eel-like *Tarrasius* of Mississippian age to the deep-bodied *Platysomus*, from the Carboniferous of Europe. *Moythomasia* (illustrated) lived among reefs of late Devonian seas. It is found in rocks of Europe and Australia.

ANCIENT LUNGFISHES

Plump-bodied fishes with a covering of shiny, circular scales. The head was broad with a blunt snout and was covered with a shiny enamel-like substance. The dorsal fins were placed far back on the body, and the pectoral and pelvic fins were long and leaf-like with scale-covered lobes.

Marine and freshwater fishes that probably fed on mollusks, using heavy tooth-plates in the jaws to crush their prey. Some were known to estivate in burrows like modern lungfishes.

Lived from Devonian to the present day, but not common now and only six species still survive. Fossils are found in rocks worldwide.

Ancient lungfishes were initially marine but later species were mainly freshwater. *Dipterus* (illustrated) was a freshwater Devonian lungfish which is found in Europe. *Uranolophus* was a similar marine fish from N. America. The six modern lungfishes are more eel-like. They can breathe air.

COELACANTHS

Medium large fishes with rounded, robust bodies covered with large circular scales. The tail is large and fan-shaped with a small terminal tuft. Posterior dorsal, anal, pectoral and pelvic fins are all mobile and used to scull the fish along. Some, like *Macropoma*, have small spines on scales and fins.

Mostly marine fishes, living in shallow water. A few lived in fresh water. Probably generally sluggish fishes but with a turn of speed provided by the deep tail. They were carnivores.

Lived from late Devonian to the present day, but only one rare species still survives. Fossils are found in rocks throughout the world.

Coelacanths were thought to have become extinct 90 million years ago, until in 1938 a living one was discovered off the Comores Is. and dubbed a "living fossil." They have not changed much through time. *Macropoma* (illustrated) is found in Cretaceous rocks in Europe; it grew up to 3ft long.

Elongated fishes, with a plump body, large head and relatively small eyes. The small pectoral and pelvic fins had a complicated internal skeleton which has been likened to the limbs of vertebrate land animals. The head and cheeks were covered with solid, ornamented, closely interlocking bones.

Mostly freshwater fishes, predators with many narrow needle-like teeth and also fangs in their long jaws. They probably lay in wait and lunged at passing prey like modern pike.

Lived from Lower Devonian to Permian times, and found in rocks of those ages throughout the world.

Eusthenopteron (illustrated) grew to about 2ft long; it had delicately ornamented, circular scales. It is found in late Devonian rocks in Europe and N. America. *Megalichthys* (from the Coal Measures of Europe) grew up to 5ft long; it had an asymmetrical tail and very thick, shiny rhomboid scales.

55

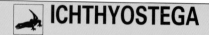

One of the oldest amphibians; it had a long body, four rather sprawling limbs and a long fish-like tail. It could move on land and had interlocking vertebrae in its backbone to support the body; its limbs were attached to the backbone by pelvic and pectoral girdles. Its head was broad with a wide mouth.

This animal lived in fresh water, fed on the animals there and laid its eggs there, but could survive short periods out of water and could move over land. It breathed air.

Lived in the late Devonian. Found in sandstones in Greenland. These rocks also contain crossopterygian fishes, confirming that they were deposited in fresh water conditions.

Eryops and *Cacops*, both later amphibians from the Permian of N. America, lacked the fish-like tail. **Seymouria**, which was a contemporary of *Eryops*, was rather more reptilian in its appearance, with a lizard-like head and a more upright stance.

56

A long flattened amphibian with small limbs. It was distinctive for its head was shaped like a boomerang, the hind parts extended backwards like bony "horns." The width of the skull was over half the length of the body of the animal, without the tail.

This amphibian spent its time at the bottom of pools and streams; its head may have acted like a hydrofoil as it swam. Its weak legs would not have supported it on land.

Lived in the Lower Permian. Found in the Texas Red Beds, which were formed in a series of deltas at the edge of the sea. Vegetation was lush, with forests of calamites and lycopods.

Diplocaulus was one of a group of similar "horned" amphibians which lived in Pennsylvanian and Permian times. In the earlier species the horns were smaller. *Trimerorhachis*, another Texas Red Bed amphibian, had a large, but normal-shaped head and broad body. It spent most of its life in water.

57

A famous fossil animal with many amphibian features in the skull, amphibian-type teeth, shoulder girdle and vertebrae. However the skull is shaped like that of a lizard, the neck vertebrae are reptilian. There are five toes on the hands and feet and it walked more like a reptile than an amphibian.

Whether *Seymouria* is truly an amphibian or a reptile depends on the kinds of eggs it laid — this is not known. Amphibians lay small eggs in water, reptiles thick-shelled ones on land.

Lived in the Lower Permian. Found in the Texas Red Beds at Seymour, Texas in the USA. It occurs too late in the geologic record to be an ancestor of reptiles.

Captorhinus was a small reptile (one foot long) from the Lower Permian of Texas and New Mexico. It was a carnivore, with long jaws and sharp teeth. It had a slender body, a long tail and long toes on the feet. Its stance was less sprawling than that of an amphibian — its legs were brought more beneath the body.

A heavily built amphibian with a broad flat head and a thick skull. It had short stout limbs, four toes on the forelimbs and five toes on the hind limbs. There were bony knobs in its skin, a protection against predators.

Eryops lived in swampy areas and probably spent a lot of time on land, like a modern alligator. Its limbs were bent almost at right angles when it walked. It was a carnivore.

Lived in the Lower Permian. Found in the Texas Red Beds, which were formed in a series of deltas at the edge of the sea. Vegetation was lush, with forests of calamites and lycopods.

Cacops was similar but only about 15in long. It had bony armor and was probably more terrestrial than *Eryops*.

SCUTOSAURUS

8ft long

A primitive early reptile with sprawling heavy limbs and short broad feet to support its heavy body. It was about the size of a bull. Its head was large and grotesque with warty protruberances.

A slow harmless reptile which fed on plants — its small serrated teeth were ideal for slicing soft vegetation. It lived in swampy or marshy areas.

Lived in Upper Permian. Found in Europe and Russia. *Scutosaurus* is often fossilized the right way up, when the animal became trapped in the swampy mud where it lived.

Pareiasaurus was a similar massive species from S. Africa and Russia. It grew up to 9ft long. It lacked the warty protruberances on the skull, which were characteristic of *Scutosaurus*.

60

The bodies of turtles are enclosed in a protective, box-like structure that may be bony or made of flexible horn. The legs are flipper-like in marine forms, short and with claws in land forms. All but Triassic turtles have a horny beak and could withdraw the head and limbs within the shell.

Turtles have lived mostly in the tropics and subtropics. The majority have lived in the sea, in swamps and in other aquatic environments; some have lived on land.

First appeared in Triassic times and still surviving, almost unchanged. Remains of turtles are found in rocks all over the world. They may be abundant, as in the badlands of S. Dakota.

Archelon (illustrated) was one of the largest turtles that ever lived, growing up to 12ft long. It lived in Cretaceous seas and is now found in Kansas Chalk. *Proganochelys* was a Triassic turtle, found in Europe, that had spines on neck and limbs. It could not retract its head beneath its shell.

Placodus (1)

was a typical placodont, a slow-moving, marine reptile that grew up to about 7ft long. It had a stout body with a short neck, a long tail & powerful, paddle-like limbs. The body was enclosed in a "basket" of ribs & the back was armored by nodules of bone. It lived on the bottom of shallow seas & ate mollusks that it picked off the sea floor. It picked up the mollusks with peg-like front teeth that protruded from its jaws. The shells were then crushed with its broad, flat, plate-like cheek teeth.

Nothosaurs (2)

Small or medium-sized marine reptiles that lived in the Triassic. They had elongated bodies and long necks. Their heads were small with long jaws & many teeth; they fed on fishes, which they could catch with their flexible necks. These animals had limbs with webbed hands & feet. They swam by paddling through the water & could probably come out onto land, like modern seals. They were smaller than the later **plesiosaurs**, which they resembled, growing about 4ft long.

Up to **50ft** long

Large marine reptiles with broad, flat bodies, long necks and limbs modified into paddles. They had small heads with sharp teeth. Some of them had long beaks while others had short snouts.

These animals "rowed" themselves along in the sea with their paddle-like limbs. They could probably move on land like a modern seal. They fed on fish.

Lived in Jurassic and Cretaceous times. Found in marine rocks in many parts of the world. Many excellent skeletons exist in museums.

Jurassic plesiosaurs like *Plesiosaurus* and *Muraenosaurus* are common in European rocks. *Elasmosaurus* (illustrated) is a Cretaceous form from Kansas; even for a plesiosaur it had an extremely long neck. **Nothosaurs** lived in the Triassic; they had shorter necks and less paddle-like limbs.

Marine fish-like reptiles with short bodies, fore and hind limbs changed to paddles, a fish-like tail and dorsal fin. They had long jaws with many teeth and large eyes.

Completely adapted for life in the ocean, they fed on fishes and were excellent swimmers. They bore their young alive — the skeletons of developing young have been found inside females.

Lived from Triassic-Cretaceous times, but most common in the Jurassic. Found in black shales in many parts of the world. In some fossils the body outline can be seen as well as bones.

Triassic ichthyosaurs like *Mixosaurus* from Nevada, had long tapering tails rather than fish-like tails. Later Jurassic and Cretaceous ichthyosaurs were all very similar, like *Ichthyosaurus* illustrated. They all died out well before the end of the Cretaceous.

Huge marine lizards with elongated bodies and tails. They had long heads with many sharp teeth in the long jaws, and short necks. Their limbs were paddle-like and the tail was flattened from side to side to form a scull.

Mosasaurs swam like crocodiles, by undulating their bodies from side to side; their limbs were used for steering. They fed on fishes and probably on other marine vertebrates.

Lived in Upper Cretaceous. Found in marine rocks throughout the world; most common in Kansas Chalk in N. America and in northern Europe.

Tylosaurus (illustrated) was over 30ft long. It is found in Upper Cretaceous rocks in N. America, Aigialosaurs, from the early Cretaceous, were small marine lizards with rather paddle-like limbs and a powerful tail. They probably only spent part of their time in the sea.

Ancient reptiles like crocodiles. They were heavily armored with long bodies and tails; the hind limbs were longer than the forelimbs and both were held beneath the body. The head was large with long jaws and many sharp teeth, and the nostrils were situated on a bump on the top of the head.

Phytosaurs lived in rivers and lakes, probably floating just beneath the surface of the water. They could probably walk on land like crocodiles. They were predators, feeding on fishes.

Lived in Upper Triassic times, and are common in rocks of this period. Found in N. America and Europe but not in the southern continents.

Rutiodon (illustrated) was a typical phytosaur; it is found in Europe and N. America. The aetosaurs were similar reptiles encased in bony armored plates. *Desmatosuchus* was a large American aetosaur with a blunt head and spikes of armor projecting out from its sides.

A small light dinosaur with hollow bones. It was bipedal in stance, with long hind legs and a long tail which counterbalanced the body. It had a long flexible neck with a small head, large eyes, and long jaws with many sharp teeth. Its forelimbs were small and had grasping hands with long claws.

This dinosaur was swift and agile, running on its hind legs. It was a predator, chasing small prey, catching them with its hands and tearing the flesh with its sharp teeth.

Lived in Upper Triassic. Found in N. America. Many skeletons, from individuals of all different ages were found at one locality in New Mexico, where they must have died together.

Ornitholestes was a similar dinosaur from N. America, which lived from late Jurassic to late Cretaceous times. It had longer fore limbs than *Coelophysis*, with three long flexible fingers and sharp claws. *Ornithomimus* from the Cretaceous, was 8ft long; it had even longer fingers and toothless jaws.

TYRANNOSAURUS

47ft long; **19ft** high

A large heavy dinosaur, probably weighing about 8 tons. It was bipedal in stance, with strong heavy hind limbs and a massive body counterbalanced by a heavy tail. It had tiny forelimbs. The skull was huge, with long massive jaws and large dagger-like teeth. The neck was short to support the head.

A huge predator and scavenger. Probably too big to chase prey very far. They may have lain in wait and relied on surprise. Teeth and claws were used to kill and dismember the prey.

Lived in Upper Cretaceous. Found in N. America, in Montana and Wyoming.

Carnosaurs were the largest land-living carnivores ever. The related *Allosaurus* has been found in the Jurassic rocks of midwestern N. America. It was about 34ft long and its fore limbs, although small, were powerful with three large claws. *Megalosaurus* was a similar dinosaur from Europe.

PLATEOSAURUS

A large clumsy dinosaur with strong heavy hind limbs, a long neck and a long tail. It was mainly bipedal in stance but dropped on to four feet, some of the time. Its forelimbs were large and its hands had four clawed fingers, the inner finger with a strong incurved claw.

This dinosaur was most likely herbivorous, browsing on tall plants. It had serrated teeth, which were probably used for shredding plants but may also have been used to tear meat.

Lived in the Upper Triassic. Found in Europe, in Germany, also France and Switzerland. In some localities, like Trössingen in Germany, it is very abundant.

Plateosaurus was a prosauropod. This was the earliest group of large herbivorous dinosaurs; they are related to the later giant sauropods. *Anchisaurus* occurs in late Triassic and early Jurassic in the Connecticut Valley, N. America. It was smaller and more slender than *Plateosaurus*, only about 8ft long.

BRONTOSAURUS

APATOSAURUS
Up to **65ft** long; about **30 tons**

A gigantic dinosaur which stood and walked on all four legs. It had a massive body and a long neck and tail; its hind limbs were longer than its forelimbs and all its feet had foot pads beneath to help support its weight. It had a small head with weak jaws and spoon-shaped teeth.

These dinosaurs probably spent some of their time in water, in rivers and swamps, feeding on lush soft vegetation. However their bodies were also adapted to take their weight on land.

Lived in Upper Jurassic. Many skeletons have been found in western and midwest N. America. At the Dinosaur National Monument in Utah, *Brontosaurus* bones can be seen *in situ*.

The sauropod dinosaurs were the largest land animals that ever lived. *Diplodocus* was 87ft long, but was slimmer and lighter than *Brontosaurus*, weighing about 10 tons; it had an extremely long neck, a small head and long whip-like tail. It comes from Upper Jurassic rocks of western N. America.

BRACHIOSAURUS

74ft long; about **75 tons**

The heaviest of all the dinosaurs, a gigantic animal. It had a very long neck with a very small head and its forelimbs were unusual in being longer than its hind limbs. Its nostrils were large and on top of its head. Its tail was much shorter than that of *Diplodocus*, and lacked the whip-like end.

Some people think this animal may have lived on land, browsing on tall trees. Others think it was aquatic or lived in swampy areas, where the water would have supported its weight.

Lived in Upper Jurassic-Lower Cretaceous times. Found in western N. America where its skeleton was preserved in river sediments. Also found in Tanzania, in east Africa.

Brachiosaurus was a sauropod dinosaur. *Camarasaurus* was similar in its generally heavy build; it had large nostrils on the top of its head and its forelimbs were a little longer than its hind limbs. However it was smaller, only 60ft long. It comes from Upper Jurassic rocks in western N. America.

A large heavy dinosaur with thick hind limbs and a thick tail. The forelimbs were small with distinctive thumb spikes; the fingers had flattened claws. The hind limbs had broad feet with three toes. It had a large head with a distinct snout; and the neck was quite short to support the head.

Iguanodon was bipedal in stance, walking on its hind limbs with its body balanced by its large heavy tail. It was herbivorous.

Lived in Lower Cretaceous. Found in large numbers in Europe, including Germany, Belgium and England. Also occurs in Asia and north Africa.

Several related dinosaurs are found in Cretaceous rocks in Europe, N. America and Africa. *Camptosaurus* (from N. America) grew up to 23ft long; it had four toes on its hind feet and no thumb spikes. *Ouranosaurus* was a strange dinosaur from Africa, with a "sail" on its back and a broad flattened snout.

A very small, agile, fast-moving dinosaur, bipedal in stance with long hind limbs and a short stiff tail which it used for balance as it ran. Its forelimbs were smaller. It had a short thick neck, cheek pouches in its mouth and broad, chisel-like, sharp teeth.

This was a herbivorous dinosaur; its teeth and cheek pouches provided it with an effective method for grinding its plant food. It could run fast to avoid predators.

Lived in Lower Cretaceous. Many whole skeletons have been found on the Isle of Wight, off the south coast of England.

There were many small hypsilophodont dinosaurs in Jurassic and Cretaceous times. *Dryosaurus*, from western USA, was similar to *Hypsilophodon*. *Tenontosaurus* (from southwestern USA) lived in the Cretaceous. It was bigger and heavier than most hypsilophodonts, up to 20ft long, and walked on all fours.

These large dinosaurs are common in the fossil record of Upper Cretaceous rocks in N. America, central & S. America, Europe & Asia. All those illustrated come from western N. America.

These dinosaurs were similar to **Iguanodon** in body & stance but the feature that gives them their name is the shape of the jaws — these were broad & flat & resembled a duck-like beak. Inside the mouth there were up to several hundred flat teeth which formed a kind of mill for grinding plant food — these were herbivorous animals.

Many of the duck-billed dinosaurs had more or less complex crests on the tops of their heads. It is not clear what function the crests served, but the nasal passage from the nostrils to the back of the throat passed through the crest. The animals may have had distinctive calls, with the crests acting as resonating devices.

Anatosaurus (**1**) was a crestless form that grew up to 30ft long.

Saurolophus (**2**) had a bony ridge on top of the head, ending in a spike at the back of the skull.

DUCK-BILLED DINOSAURS

Corythosaurus (**3**) had a high, helmet-shaped crest on its head.

Parasaurolophus (**4**) was the most extraordinary, with a tubular hollow crest that extended 3ft behind the skull.

The exact mode of life of the duck-billed dinosaurs is a subject of debate. They may have lived semi-aquatic lives, for they had webbed hands & feet & a flattened tail which could have been used for swimming. Their bones are often found in rocks formed from sediments deposited along rivers & lakes. However their strong backbone

& hind limbs indicates a life on land. They may have lived in herds along the banks of rivers, since their bones are often numerous.

Several nests of the duck-billed dinosaur, *Maiasaura*, have been found in Montana, USA. Some of the nests contain egg fragments, others contain large young, suggesting that the young remained in the nest for some time after hatching & that the dinosaurs cared for their young. The nests show signs that the mothers returned to the same site, year after year.

PROTOCERATOPS

A small dinosaur with a large head and a bony frill overhanging the neck at the back of the head. It had a bulky body with a thick tail and walked on all fours. Its mouth had a sharp parrot-like beak and its brows were thickened above the eyes.

A herbivorous dinosaur which laid eggs in concentric circles in depressions in sand. The nests have been fossilized.

Lived in Upper Cretaceous. Found in the Gobi Desert, Mongolia. It is famous for the nests, eggs and many skeletons of hatchlings, juveniles and adults that have been found.

Most other related dinosaurs (ceratopians) had horns on their heads. *Montanoceratops* was similar to *Protoceratops* but had one horn; its fossil remains are found in Montana, in N. America.

30ft long

A large, heavy dinosaur which walked on all fours. It had a deep bulky body with a large head and a short bony frill overhanging the neck at the back of the head. It had three horns, two above the eyes and a shorter one on the snout. The mouth had a sharp parrot-like beak.

A herbivorous dinosaur which probably lived in herds. Young animals and females may have been defended by the males which could form a ring around them, horns facing outwards.

Lived in the Upper Cretaceous. Found in N. America; many have been found in Wyoming, in the Red Deer River Valley and in Colorado.

All ceratopian dinosaurs lived in the Upper Cretaceous. Some had long frills at the back of the neck, eg. *Chasmosaurus* (from western USA) had a frill which extended well beyond its shoulders. *Centrosaurus* (a short-frilled type) had spines and two horns on the edges of its frill, and a horn on the snout.

DEINONYCHUS

10ft long

A small agile, predatory dinosaur which may have hunted in packs. It had long hind limbs, a large head with many sharp teeth and a long stiff tail. Its forelimbs were long with grasping hands and long claws. Its most extraordinary feature was the sickle-shaped claw on the second toe of each hind foot.

This dinosaur apparently killed by grasping its prey with its forelimbs while kicking and disembowelling it with the huge claws on the hind feet. Teeth were used to shear the meat.

Lived in Upper Cretaceous. Found in N. America, in southern Montana. Several almost complete skeletons have been found.

Dromaeosaurus comes from Upper Cretaceous rocks in the Red Deer River Valley of Canada. Only fragmentary remains have been found but we know that it was about 6ft long, with a large head, long fore limbs with grasping clawed hands, and a sickle-shaped claw on the second toe of its hind feet.

6ft long

A small dinosaur with a massive domed head. It was bipedal in stance, probably with a long tail. Only partial skeletons have been found so far, hands and feet are still missing so this reconstruction is partly conjectural.

A herbivorous dinosaur which may have lived like mountain sheep or goats do today. Seniority in a herd may have been decided by head butting.

Lived in the Upper Cretaceous. Found in the western states of the USA; Montana, S. Dakota and Wyoming.

The related *Pachycephalosaurus*, from Montana, is known from its skull alone. It was probably bigger than *Stegoceras*, up to 26ft long, with a massively thickened skull and small knobs on the back of the head and on the snout.

A large dinosaur with a bulky body and a characteristic double row of large bony plates along the back, down to the tail. The short tail had four spikes. It walked on all fours. It had a small narrow head with a toothless beak.

A herbivorous dinosaur. The skin over the plates may have been used for heat regulation, absorbing heat when the plates were facing the sun and losing heat when they were turned end on.

Lived in the Lower Jurassic. Found in N. America, in Wyoming and Colorado. Several complete skeletons are known.

Stegosaurid dinosaurs lived in Jurassic and Cretaceous times. They are found in N. America, Europe, Asia and Africa. *Kentrosaurus*, from the Jurassic of Tanzania, had plates on its back but these became spike-like on the rear of its body and tail. *Tuojiangosaurus*, from southern China, had conical plates.

20ft long

A heavily armored dinosaur which walked on all fours. It had a short thick neck with a broad, flattened head and back, protected by sheets of bone and spines. The end of its tail was armed with a heavy bony club. It had short sturdy legs to support the heavy body.

The armor was formed of plates of bone, rather than a single sheet, which gave the animal flexibility. It could probably move quite fast and defend itself with its tail club.

Lived in the Upper Cretaceous. Found in the Red Deer River Valley of Alberta, Canada. Several skulls, partial skeletons and body armor have been found.

This is an ankylosaur dinosaur, *Ankylosaurus*, from Alberta and Montana, grew to 33ft long. *Polacanthus*, from the early Cretaceous of southern England, had a row of spines on each side of its back and a double row of spines on its tail; it had no club on its tail.

81

1

2

Scelidosaurus (1)

Only one more or less complete skeleton has been found, in early Jurassic rocks in southern England.

This was a 13ft long, armored dinosaur, with armor extending over its back & sides, & down its tail. The armor consisted of bony studs, like that of ankylosaurs. The animal probably walked on all fours; the hind limbs were strong & heavy & had broad feet with stubby toes. Little is known of the forelimbs but it seems likely that they were also strong & heavy.

Heterodontosaurus (2)

A small bipedal dinosaur (it was only 4ft long) from Upper Triassic and Lower Jurassic rocks of S. Africa.

This dinosaur had strong hind limbs, strong forelimbs with large hands, & a long tail. It is unusual amongst dinosaurs, in that it possessed three kinds of teeth. It was a herbivore. It used its front cutting teeth to nip off leaves & ground the plants to pulp with broad ridged cheek teeth. It also had fangs, which it may have used for defense or for digging roots.

Struthiomimus (3)

These animals come from the late Cretaceous rocks of western N. America & Mongolia.

Also known as an ostrich dinosaur, this animal grew 10–13ft tall, had long hind legs, a compact body, a short stiff tail & a long neck. It could run fast. The skull bones were light & the jaws were flexible & toothless, resembling the beak of a bird. Food could probably be maneuvered easily. The forelimbs were long & slender, with three long, slender, clawed fingers.

Psittacosaurus (4)

A small dinosaur, about 6½ft long, from Upper Cretaceous rocks of Mongolia.

This dinosaur could adopt a bipedal stance or drop to all fours. It had a bulky body, a long tail and strong hind legs with heavy claws on the toes. It could use its forelegs for walking but the hands had long claws & could also be used for grasping plants. This was a herbivore, with a parrot-like hooked beak & no teeth at the front of the jaws.

RHAMPHORHYNCHUS

2ft long; wingspan about **4ft**

Flying reptile with a short body and a long tail. The fourth fingers of its forelimbs were greatly elongated to support the wing membranes. Its hind limbs were small and weak. Its head was small and borne on a long flexible neck; it had a long beak with many forwardly-pointed teeth and large eyes.

An active flyer, capable of sustained and acrobatic flight and of diving for fish in the sea. It may have walked on land like a bird, may have been warm blooded and covered with fur.

Lived in Lower Jurassic. Found in southern Germany in Bavarian slates. Found always in marine rocks so it is assumed it lived near the sea.

Eudimorphodon, a similar pterosaur from the late Triassic of Italy, had sharp teeth which did not point forward. *Pterodactylus* was only the size of a sparrow and lacked a tail. It occurs in Jurassic rocks in Europe.

PTERANODON

16ft long; wingspan **25ft**

Flying reptile with a short body and very short tail. The fourth fingers of its forelimbs were greatly elongated to support the wing membranes. Its hind limbs were small and weak. The head had a long toothless beak and an almost equally long crest at the back of the skull.

May have spent much of its time over the ocean. It fed on fish. It probably moved with difficulty on land, unbalanced by its crest. It may have been covered with fur and warm blooded.

Lived in the Upper Cretaceous. Found in the Niobrara chalk, a fine-grained marine rock, of Kansas, N. America.

Pteranodon was one of the largest pterosaurs. Recently an even larger one, named *Quetzalcoatlus*, was found in Upper Cretaceous rocks in Texas. It had a 35ft wingspan; it is the largest flying animal ever discovered.

Up to **11ft** long

A reptile like a large lizard, with a long body and strong, rather sprawling limbs. It had a large head with deep jaws, dagger-like teeth at the front of the mouth and smaller teeth at the back. It had a large sail on its back, formed from skin stretched over elongated vertebral spines.

It is thought that the sail was a device for maintaining body temperature; it provided a large surface area for heating or cooling the animal. This was an aggressive carnivore.

Lived in Lower Permian times. Found in the Texas Red Beds of N. America. These rocks were formed in a delta with lush vegetation; *Dimetrodon* is the most common reptile in the rocks.

Edaphosaurus was a similar reptile from the late Carboniferous and Permian times of Europe and N. America. It grew up to 11ft long. The spines of its sail were thicker and knobby with protruding crossbars. *Edaphosaurus* was herbivorous; it had a small head and many similar teeth.

8ft long

A large heavy reptile with a bulky body and shoulders much higher than its hips, so that the body sloped downwards from the head. It had a large head with interlocking teeth in the mouth. Its limbs were heavy with broad flat feet.

Slow-moving, heavy herbivores which lived in large herds, probably in dry areas of the land. The skull was very thick, and males may have competed for dominance by head butting.

Lived in mid Permian times. Found in S. Africa, where their fossils are common in mid Permian rocks.

Kannemeyeria comes from the early Triassic of S. Africa, S. America and Russia. It was a large, heavily built herbivore with tusks in its mouth. *Lystrosaurus*, from the Triassic of S. Africa, China, India, Russia and Antarctica, had a downturned snout and tusks. It probably lived in and around water.

87

A relatively small mammal-like reptile, with a large, rather narrow and pointed head. The jaws had incisors, large canines, and cutting teeth at the sides ("true" reptiles have only one kind of teeth.) The limbs were held beneath the body, knees pointing forward and elbows pointing backward.

Active carnivores, which could move quickly. Some scientists think they were covered in hair like mammals, although their skeletons still show reptilian features.

Lived in Lower Triassic times. Found in the Karroo Beds of South Africa; these beds in the South African desert are well-known for their fossils of mammal-like reptiles.

Thrinaxodon was about a foot long, an active carnivore, like a smaller version of *Cynognathus*. It also comes from the S. African Karroo Beds. Other related species are found in Asia, Europe and S. America.

MESOZOIC MAMMALS

Small early mammals ranging from the size of a shrew to the size of a cat. Their skeletons can be distinguished from those of mammal-like reptiles by details in the braincase, lower jaw and teeth. We assume they were fur-covered and maintained a constant body temperature.

Most of these small primitive mammals, like ***Morganucodon*** (illustrated) and *Megazostrodon* were insectivorous, catching insects and worms. Others were carnivores and herbivores.

These small mammals occur in late Triassic to Cretaceous rocks, in Europe, N. America, Asia and Africa. They survived throughout the age of dinosaurs.

Morganucodon is found in late Triassic rocks in Britain, China and Lesotho. Multituberculates are known from late Jurassic to Eocene; Triconodonts (cat-sized carnivores) lived in Jurassic and Cretaceous; Pantotheres (ancestors of modern mammals) come from the Jurassic. All occur in N. America and Europe.

Marsupials were probably found all over the world in Cretaceous times. They have survived to Recent times in isolation in Australasia and many also survived until Pleistocene times in S. America, dying out when it became joined to N. America and was invaded by the true mammals. Now only a few (the opossums) survive in the Americas. Marsupials differ from other mammals, not only in the possession of a pouch, but also in their skeleton and teeth formulae, so they can easily be identified as fossils.

South American Marsupials
Most S. American marsupials were carnivores, feeding on the slow, true mammalian herbivores living at the time. ***Borhyaena*** (**1**) was one such animal that lived in the Miocene of Patagonia; it looked like a large, rather slow dog with a long body, strong limbs & sharp claws on its feet. It had large slashing canines. ***Thylacosmilus*** (**2**) was a marsupial sabertooth cat, with saber teeth larger than any found in the true **sabertooths**. It lived in Pliocene times in Argentina.

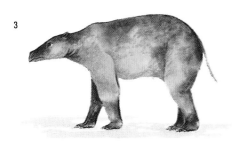

Australian marsupials

Virtually all mammals in Australia are marsupials. Modern forms parallel the true mammals, from marsupial mice to marsupial moles, wolves and cats. Kangaroos are grazing marsupials.

Neohelos (**3**) was a herbivore that lived in Miocene times. It is very common in the fossil record. It was about the size of a cow & probably lived in herds, browsing on shrubs and trees. **Palorchestes** (**4**) was also as large as a cow. It had powerful forelimbs with large claws. It lived in woodland areas, browsing on trees and shrubs, probably living a life similar to the S. American ground sloths, from late Miocene to Pleistocene times.

Australian carnivores included *Thylacoleo*, the marsupial lions of Miocene to Pleistocene times. The biggest grew to about the size of a leopard. The Tasmanian Devil, *Sarcophilus*, is still living; similar forms are known in the fossil record since the early Miocene. The Tasmanian Wolf, *Thylacinus*, has only recently become extinct.

Small mammals. They usually have small heads with long snouts and sharp teeth, fairly long bodies and long tails. They put the whole foot on the ground and the five toes have sharp claws. Modern forms include hedgehogs, shrews and moles. Hedgehogs have spines. Moles live underground.

Insectivores mostly fed on insects, worms and mollusks, although some of the larger ones, like *Deinogalerix*, were probably carnivores and scavengers.

Insectivores mostly fed on insects, worms and mollusks, although some of the larger ones, like *Deinogalerix*, were probably carnivores and scavengers.

Zalambdalestes (**1**,) an early insectivore from Mongolia, lived in late Cretaceous times; it probably jumped like an elephant shrew. *Deinogalerix* (**2**) was a giant hairy hedgehog from the Miocene; its remains are found in Italy. Hedgehogs first appeared in the Paleocene, shrews and moles in the Eocene.

HYAENODON

There were many species of *Hyaenodon*. They were carnivorous mammals, ranging from stoat-size to hyena-size with long limbs and wrists and ankles raised off the ground. They probably had dog-like claws on their toes. They had large heads, big canine teeth and shearing cheek teeth.

These were quite fast, agile hunters with stereoscopic vision to aid in their hunting of the slow-moving hoofed mammals of their day.

Lived from Eocene to Oligocene times. Many species of *Hyaenodon* are found in the White River Series, in N. America; they are also found in Eurasia and Africa.

Hyaenodon and its relatives, like the wolverine-like *Oxyaena* and fox-like *Sinopa*, were early carnivores known as creodonts. They are believed to have been slower than modern carnivores, and to have died out as these faster hunters and the later faster-moving hoofed mammals evolved together.

AMPHICYON

4ft tall to shoulders

A large heavy dog, more like a bear in build than a dog. It had a heavy body and short powerful limbs with wrists and ankles raised off the ground. The feet had five spreading toes. The head was wolf-like and it had a long heavy tail.

These big dogs were probably scavengers, too large and heavy to chase prey. Their teeth are not those of a pure carnivore; their crushing molars may have been used to break bones.

Lived from Eocene to Pliocene times. Found in Europe. Several species of *Amphicyon* are found in N. America, Asia and Africa.

These animals are sometimes known as Bear-dogs. True dogs are lighter in build with longer legs; modern dogs are plains dwellers, living in packs and able to run fast. True bears are heavy bodied with teeth adapted for an omnivorous diet, and their tails are reduced to stubs.

A large lion-like cat, distinguished by its canine teeth. The upper canines were extremely long and curved while the lower canines were small. Powerful face muscles ensured that the mouth could be opened to 90°, to facilitate the action of the canines.

Slow-moving cats which preyed on mastodonts and elephants; they became extinct at the same time as these animals. The long canines were used for stabbing, slashing and slicing.

Smilodon lived in the Pleistocene, in North and South America; its remains are especially common at the Rancho La Brea tar pits in California.

Smilodon was one of many sabertooths that lived in Europe, and N. and S. America from Oligocene to Pleistocene times. Scimitar tooth cats lived in the Pleistocene of Europe; they had shorter canines and very long forelimbs. ***Thylacosmilus*** was a marsupial sabertooth which lived in S. America.

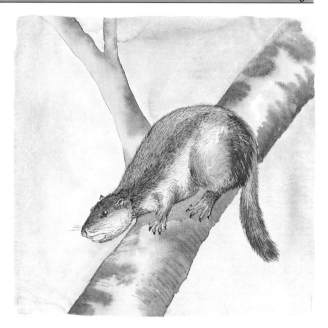

A squirrel-like rodent and one of the earliest known. It had a long low skull and chisel-like gnawing incisors. It walked on all fours, using the claws on its toes for grasping and climbing; its hind legs were longer than its front ones. It had a long tail for balance.

These small rodents scampered about on the ground and climbed into bushes. They fed on roots and nuts, using their gnawing incisors for feeding.

Lived from Paleocene to Eocene times. Found in N. America, in the Wasatch Formations of Wyoming and New Mexico.

Rodents can be distinguished from insectivores like *Zalambdalestes*, by their incisors and by details in skull and skeleton. The more primitive mammals, like *Morganucodon*, also lack the gnawing incisors and occur much earlier in the fossil record.

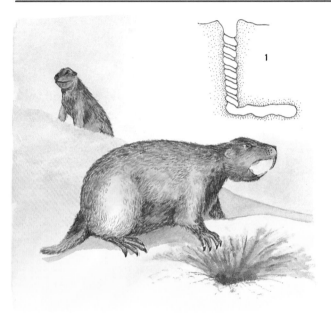

A burrowing beaver. Like all rodents, it had only one pair of gnawing incisors in upper and lower jaws. It could run on all fours, and stand upright on its hind legs like a gopher. The forelimbs had grasping hands, the hind feet were long and flat. There were claws on the fingers and toes.

This beaver made distinctive burrows. Each consisted of a horizontal living chamber below ground and a vertical corkscrew-like spiral tunnel from the surface to the chamber.

Lived in the Miocene. Found in Nebraska, USA, where the fossilized burrows resist erosion (**1**) and stand out against the bluffs above the Upper Niobrara River.

Castoroides was a Pleistocene giant beaver (adults were as big as a black bear) from the USA and Canada. It had short legs and webbed feet, was probably a powerful swimmer which lived in lakes and ponds. *Steneofiber* was a similar beaver from the early Miocene of central France.

A tank-like mammal with a dome-like carapace of armor on its back. It had a short armored tail and sturdy legs with short toes and hoofed claws. The head was large with deep jaws and face, and was covered with a bony helmet.

A herbivore which could grind up tough grasses with its cheek teeth. It may have lived near water, since its remains often occur with those of capybaras, which live near water today.

Lived in the Pleistocene. Found in Argentina, S. America.

Glyptodonts lived from the Miocene to the Pleistocene in S. America. Some had spiky tails, others had tails that were armored but not spiky. They migrated northwards into central America and lived as far north as Texas and Florida till the end of the Pleistocene, when they became extinct.

A very large heavy mammal with broad heavy leg bones to take the weight of the animal, large feet and enormous curved claws. The claws on the third toes were especially large. The head was large and the teeth, which were only present on the sides of the mouth, were peg-like and high-crowned.

Ground sloths walked on the sides of the hind feet and on the knuckles of the forefeet. They probably browsed on leaves of bushes and may have used their claws for digging roots.

Lived in the Pleistocene. Found in Patagonia, S. America and north to the Carolinas in N. America.

Ground sloths existed in S. America from Oligocene to Pleistocene and invaded N. America in the Pleistocene. *Megatherium* was one of the biggest. *Megalonyx* lived as far north as Alaska. *Nothrotheriops* has been found preserved in caves in southwest USA, with hair still remaining on the skeletons.

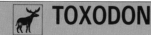

A large heavy mammal, like a cross between a rhino and a guinea pig, with a capacious body and short heavy limbs to support its weight. The feet were broad, with three toes and hooves. The ears and nostrils were high on its head.

It probably fed on the leaves of shrubs and grasses. Its teeth were high-crowned and grew throughout its life, to compensate for wear by the hard grasses.

Lived in the Pliocene and Pleistocene. Found in the Pampas of S. America where it was the commonest large hoofed mammal in the Pleistocene. First discovered by Charles Darwin.

Toxodonts were a group of mammals that appeared in Eocene times, became common in the Oligocene and Miocene and extinct in the Pleistocene. Representatives include *Nesodon* (Miocene), which resembled a hornless rhino and *Homaladotherium*, which used its clawed feet to pull down branches on which it browsed.

6ft tall at shoulders

A camel-like mammal, but unrelated to the camels. It had a long neck and legs and three hoofed toes on each foot. Its head was long, probably with a flexible proboscis. It had high-crowned cheek teeth in the jaws.

A herbivore which probably browsed on the leaves of shrubs and trees. Its long legs enabled it to run away from predators.

Lived in Pliocene and Pleistocene times, in Argentina.

One of a whole group of mammals (the litopterns) only found in S. America. They first appeared in the Paleocene and the last survivors became extinct at the end of the Pleistocene. *Thesodon*, a litoptern from the Miocene of S. America, was smaller and more slender.

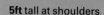

UINTATHERIUM

5ft tall at shoulders

A large hoofed mammal, grotesque in appearance and ponderous in movement. It had a heavy body, short limbs and broad spreading feet. The head was very strange, with six horns pointing in different directions. The males had large protruding canine teeth.

A herbivore, probably browsing on leaves of shrubs and trees. The large canines of the males may not have been used for feeding, but for contesting dominance.

Lived in the mid Eocene. Found in western N. America, in the Washakie and Bridger beds of Wyoming.

Uintatherium was a member of the group of mammals known as uintatheres. They were amongst the earliest of the hoofed mammals and died out by the end of the Oligocene. Other uintatheres were mostly smaller than *Uintatherium* and lacked horns.

A horse-like mammal, with a barrel-shaped body and a horse-like head. However its forelegs were longer than its hind legs so that it had a sloping back, and its feet ended, not in hooves, but in claws. There were three claws on each foot.

A herbivore which may have used its clawed feet for digging roots out of the ground. It may also have browsed on branches pulled down by its long forelegs. Lived in woodland savannah.

Lived in the Miocene. Found in N. America. A large number of bones are found in the Agate Bone Bed, south of Harrison, Nebraska, where the animals were killed in a flash flood.

The chalicotheres (the group to which *Moropus* belongs) lived from the Eocene to Pleistocene times in N. America, Asia and Africa. *Chalicotherium* (from Kenya) became extinct in Pleistocene times. It had short hind legs and longer forelegs with inwardly curved claws, so that it walked on its knuckles.

The largest ever land mammal. It had long straight legs, with the front legs longer than the hind legs, and a long neck. Its head was about 4ft long but was still small in proportion to the body.

This animal probably browsed on trees like a modern giraffe. It could reach into tall trees with its long legs and neck.

Lived in Oligocene and early Miocene. Found in Pakistan, northwest India, and Mongolia.

Baluchitherium was a rhinoceros. *Caenopus* was an early hornless rhino from the Oligocene of N. America; it was only 5ft tall at the shoulders. The Woolly Rhinoceros lived in the arctic in Pleistocene times; it was covered in long dense hair and had two horns. It was often illustrated in cave paintings.

A large heavy mammal, like a modern rhino, with a capacious body, short massive limbs and broad feet with stubby toes. The skull had a characteristic "dip" in the top and there was a pair of nasal "horns" on the nose, larger in the males than in the females, and probably used in fights for dominance.

These animals fed on soft vegetation, which grew in Oligocene times. With the spread of the grasses in the Miocene, the softer plants became rarer and the animals became extinct.

Lived in the Oligocene. Found in N. America, in the White River Series. These rocks form a series of isolated badland outcrops, which occur from Colorado to Saskatchewan.

Titanotheres (of which *Brontotherium* was one of the latest and heaviest) lived in N. America in Eocene and Oligocene times, reaching Asia in the Oligocene. Earlier forms were smaller. *Palaeosyops* (from the Eocene of N. America) lived in forest areas; it had no horns.

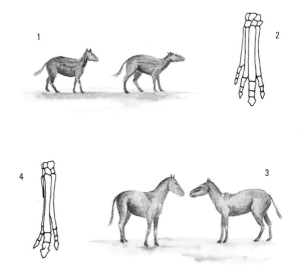

There is an extraordinarily complete fossil record of the evolution of horses in N. America, where they evolved. This is because the complete sequence of rocks from Eocene times to Recent times is present on the continent and because the bones of horses fossilize well.

The earliest known horse is **Eohippus** (**1**,) from the early Eocene. It was only as big as a fox, with a small head, a short face & low-crowned teeth. It was a fast runner with long slender limbs, & wrists & ankles raised off the ground so that its toes were almost vertical. It had three hoofed toes on the hind feet, four on the fore feet (**2**.) It lived in woods & savannahs, browsing on the vegetation.

Mesohippus (**3**) lived in the Oligocene. It was about the size of a sheep & had three toes on each foot (**4**.) Its head was longer than that of *Eohippus* & it had complex cheek teeth on each side of its mouth to grind the drier vegetation of the Oligocene period. However it was still a browsing animal.

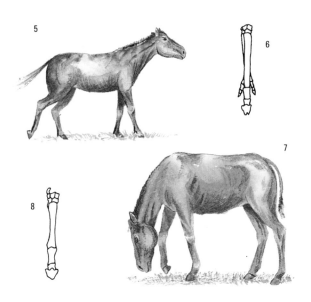

Merychippus (5) lived in the Miocene & was a true grazing horse, feeding on prairie grasses (grasses first appeared in the Miocene). Its limbs were longer than those of the earlier horses, & the shin bones were fused to strengthen the limbs for galloping; however it still had three toes (6.) Its head was deeper with tall cheek teeth. The teeth had elaborate surfaces for grinding tough grasses. Many extinct species, like the Hipparions, evolved from these horses, as well as *Pliohippus* & the modern horses.

Pliohippus (7) appeared in late Miocene. It was similar to *Merychippus* but had only one toe on each foot (8) & longer legs.

Equus (the modern horse) continued these trends. It has longer legs, a deeper head, more elaborate teeth and a bigger brain than the earlier horses. Modern horses appeared in N. America in the Pliocene & then invaded Eurasia & Africa. They died out in N. America in the Pleistocene (about 8000 years ago,) & were re-introduced into the New World by men.

ARCHAEOTHERIUM

over **3ft** tall at shoulders

A large pig-like mammal, like a wild boar. It had rather humped shoulders but it had a straight back and long legs, both adaptations for running. It only had two toes on each hoofed foot. It had a very large head with an elongated face, knobs on the lower jaw and a flange on each cheek bone.

An omnivorous animal, with stout incisors and large canine teeth. It probably fed on ground plants, roots and cones, also on carcasses as a scavenger. It lived in forest regions.

Lived in the Oligocene. Found in the White River Series of rocks, where they outcrop as badlands in Nebraska and S. Dakota, of N. America.

Archaeotherium belonged to a group of pig-like mammals called enteledonts, which lived in the Oligocene in N. America and Europe, becoming extinct in early Miocene. *Dinohyus*, from N. America, was as large as a bison; it was probably a scavenger and also ate plants. *Entelodon* lived in forests in Europe.

16in tall at shoulders

A sheep-like mammal with short limbs and four toes on each foot. It had teeth like the modern ruminants (cows and deer) and has been called "ruminating swine," but it also had canines.

These animals roamed the woods and plains of N. America in large herds. They were herbivores, browsing on shrubs and small plants.

Lived in the Oligocene. Thousands of skeletons have been found in the Oreodon beds in the White River badlands of S. Dakota. Remains are also found in other Oligocene rocks in N. America.

One of a large group of New World mammals, the oreodonts, common from early Oligocene to Pliocene times. They were very successful and *Merycoidodon* (originally called *Oreodon*) was one of the most abundant. Some of them, like *Brachycrus* from the Miocene, had a tapir-like snout.

109

Often called a giraffe-camel. A mammal with a very long neck and long stilt-like legs, terminating in two hoofed toes on each foot. The lower incisors were spoon-shaped and worked against a horny pad in the upper jaw — an ideal system for cropping plants.

This animal browsed on the leaves of high trees. It probably lived in savannah country with clumps of trees in wide grassy plains. It could run fast to avoid predators.

Lived from the mid Miocene to Pliocene times. Found in N. America, from the mid Miocene of Montana to the Pliocene of Nebraska, Nevada and Colorado.

Camels first appeared in the late Eocene. They were once much more diverse and numerous than they are today, particularly in N. America. Eocene camels were small (rabbit-size) but camels were bigger in the Miocene and similar to modern llamas; they were adapted to the grasslands. Only modern camels have humps.

A deer-like mammal, the males distinguished by a pair of long, backwardly directed horns above the eyes and a long, forked, Y-shaped horn on the nose. They had long legs with cloven hooves. They had no upper incisors in the mouth, instead there was a horny pad for cropping vegetation.

These were grazing animals of grassland areas, with long legs adapted for fast, long-distance running. The horns were probably used by the males for dominance competitions.

Lived from the late Miocene to Pliocene times. Found in N. America.

Similar animals included *Syndyoceras*, from the Upper Miocene of N. America, which had curved horns above the eyes and two divergent V-shaped horns on the nose; and *Kyptoceras*, from the Pleistocene, which had curved, forwardly pointing horns above the eyes and a pair of inwardly-curved nasal horns.

111

GIANT IRISH ELK

MEGALOCEROS
6ft tall at shoulders

A giant deer. The males had huge palmate antlers, the largest measuring 10ft across and weighing 100lbs. The antlers were lost each year and regrew the following year (as in all deer.) They had no upper incisors in the mouth, instead there was a horny pad for cropping vegetation.

These were browsing animals of woodland areas, with long legs adapted for fast, long-distance running. The horns were probably used by the males for dominance competitions.

Lived in the Pleistocene. Skeletons are found in large numbers in Irish bogs, although the animals' range actually extended from Ireland eastwards through Siberia to China.

One of many deer found in the Pleistocene and Recent times. *Eucladoceras* was the Pleistocene bush-antlered deer which lived in Europe; it had 12 tines or branches on each antler. The Giant American Moose lived in the Pleistocene.

112

A large heavily built mammal, related to modern giraffes but more like an ox in build with a heavy body. It had relatively slender legs however, with cloven hooves. It had four horns, two very large spreading ones on the top of the head and two smaller ones above the eyes.

A browsing animal with low-crowned cheek teeth. The upper incisor teeth were replaced by a horny pad, as in many of these animals. It lived in woodland and forested areas.

Lived in the Pleistocene. Found in India. Sivatheres as a group are found in Europe, Asia and Africa. Bronze figurines, apparently of sivatheres, are known from ancient Sumeria.

Modern giraffes have long legs and necks, and two horns on their heads; they browse on tall trees. The modern Okapi, from the Belgian Congo, is very similar to earlier giraffid animals like *Palaeotragus* from the Pliocene and *Giraffokeryx* from the Miocene and Pliocene. Both are found in S. Eurasia and Africa.

Modern elephants are the only survivors of a once world-wide group of large herbivores (which includes the mammoth illustrated on the opposite page) that first appeared in the Eocene.

Early forms like the Oligocene *Moeritherium* (**1**,) were about the size of a pygmy hippo & probably lived in & around water. *Moeritherium* had a heavy body, short stout legs & spreading feet with flat hooves on the ends of the toes. It had small tusks in the mouth & probably had a flexible snout. It is found in Egypt & the Sahara.

Deinotherium (**2**) lived in the Miocene & Pliocene of Eurasia & Pleistocene of Africa. It stood 10ft high at the shoulders, had long straight legs & a long trunk. It had no tusks in the upper jaws, but two long downwardly curving tusks in the lower jaws may have been used to dig roots or pull up plants.

Gomphotherium (**3**) was an early true elephant from the Miocene of Eurasia, Africa & N. America. It was nearly as tall as an Indian Elephant, had a long trunk & four straight tusks, two in the upper & two in the lower jaw.

A large woolly "elephant" with dense dark hair and a thick hair undercoat. There was a 3in layer of fat beneath the hair to protect the animal from the cold. It had a heavy body with a long sloping back, long straight legs, a high-domed head and a long trunk. There was a pair of tusks in the lower jaw.

The mammoths fed on tundra grasses and plants in summer, shrubs in winter. They were hunted by paleolithic man with pit fall traps and commonly illustrated in cave paintings.

Lived in the Pleistocene. Found in northern areas of N. America, Europe and Asia. Carcasses have been recovered from ice crevasses. They died out in Siberia only 12,000 years ago.

The American Mammoth lived in Pleistocene times in southern N. America. It grew to 14ft tall or more and had long curved tusks. The American Mastodont (Pliocene-Pleistocene) had long straight tusks, curved slightly at the tips. Mastodonts are found at the Rancho La Brea tar pits, in California.

An early upright man with a large head, relative to body size, and a hairy body. The skull was massive and very rugged with large broad molar teeth in the jaws. *Australopithecus* walked only on its feet but it had very long arms, which it may have used for balancing, when squatting.

These men probably lived in roving troops, like modern baboons. Their hands were capable of grasping, and they almost certainly used sticks, if not more sophisticated tools.

Lived in the Pliocene, around 3 million years ago. Found in South and East Africa; their remains were first found in caves in the Transvaal.

These men are also known as Robust Australopithecines, from their rugged skulls. Gracile Australopithecines lived in South and East Africa at the same time; they were about 5ft tall with smaller teeth, and there were also differences in the pelvic bones of the two kinds of men.

Shorter than modern man with a projecting jaw but no chin, and a receding forehead. It had a larger brain than modern man, swept back cheek bones and massive eyebrow ridges. It was more or less upright in stance, stocky and robust in stature, with opposite thumbs on the hands and modern man-type feet.

They lived in caves and shelters, wore skins, and used tools — scrapers, knives and hand axes. They hunted the Pleistocene mammals like woolly rhinos, mammoths, giant elk etc.

Found in the Mousterian period of the last interglacial of the Pleistocene and into the last glacial period, in Europe, around the Mediterranean, western Asia and northern Africa.

Homo erectus is known from fragmentary remains from Java, Africa, Europe and China; these men were skilful hunters, used hand axes and had fixed campsites. Early *Homo sapiens* was taller, used more sophisticated tools and made animal paintings on the walls of caves.

 # BASILOSAURUS

70ft long

A giant early whale, slim and elongated in shape. Its tail was transformed into a horizontal fluke. It had no hind limbs and the forelimbs were fin-like and used as paddles. The blow-hole was situated half-way along the head. This was a toothed whale with cheek teeth which were flattened and serrated.

These were marine mammals, completely adapted to a life in the ocean, except that they still breathed air. They swam by powerful vertical flexing of the tail and fed on fishes.

Lived in the Upper Eocene. Found in N. America, in marine rocks widespread in southeastern USA; also found in Egypt in N. Africa.

Toothed whales (eg. dolphins, sperm whales) appeared in Oligocene times; they have many teeth and feed on fishes. Whalebone whales (eg. blue whales) appeared in the Miocene; they use a straining apparatus (the whalebone) to feed on plankton. They grow larger than toothed whales.

This early bird had a dinosaur-like skeleton with a bird-like skull and teeth in the jaws. The long tail had two rows of feathers along its sides and the long forelimb formed a feathered wing, with three clawed fingers. The hind feet had the first toe rotated backwards, as in all birds.

Obviously this bird could glide but its powers of flapping flight are a question of debate. It walked on its hind legs.

Lived in Upper Jurassic. Found at Solnhofen, in Bavaria in a rare fine-grained limestone deposited in shallow marine lagoons. Feathers were preserved as impressions in the rock.

Archaeopteryx can be distinguished from dinosaurs by the feathers, the bird-like features of its skull and the rotated first toes of its feet. It is different to modern birds in its possession of teeth, in its long tail with many vertebrae and its lack of a keel bone for the attachment of flight muscles.

Like a modern bird, this animal had light bones, a keel bone, pelvic bones fused to the vertebrae, a rotated first toe in the hind feet and a forelimb modified as a wing. It had no clawed fingers on the wing. It had a short tail with a fan of feathers. However it probably had teeth in its jaws.

A flying bird, probably like a modern tern. This was a marine bird which could fly actively and which fed on fishes.

One of several birds preserved in the Upper Cretaceous, fine-grained Niobrara Chalk in Kansas, USA. This marine environment was conducive to the fossilization of birds.

Birds are rare in the fossil record, not because they are rare organisms, but because their fragile bones do not fossilize, they soon break up and disintegrate. *Hesperornis*, also from the Niobrara Chalk, was a flightless diving bird, like a loon. It had weak forelimbs and no keel bone.

Up to **10ft** tall

A huge flightless bird, with a large body covered in downy feathers. It had strong legs and four large clawed toes on each foot. It could probably run fast on these legs like modern ostriches.

Fossilized eggs of *Aepyornis* are still found in the sand on the coast of Madagascar or washed ashore. They are about 2½ft around the longest circumference. Some eggs contain embryos.

Lived in Pleistocene and Recent times. Found in Madagascar. This may have been the Giant Roc in the tales of Sinbad the Sailor.

Fragments of similar birds and eggs are found elsewhere in Africa. Moas were huge flightless birds found in New Zealand. They had no wings, but were fast runners with long, strong hind limbs. The largest was nearly 12ft tall. They were hunted by Maoris and became extinct in the last few hundred years.

INDEX

Illustrated species are in bold.

Latin names of animals and plants are in italics. Common names, and names of groups and families are in ordinary type. Often prehistoric animals and plants only have a Latin name; in many cases the Latin name has become a common name, as in *Tyrannosaurus*, for instance.